W9-AMP-838

HELPING OTHERS

By Steffi Cavell-Clarke

Crabtree Publishing Company

www.crabtreebooks.com

1-800-387-7650

Published in Canada
Crabtree Publishing
616 Welland Avenue
St. Catharines, ON
L2M 5V6

Published in the United States
Crabtree Publishing
PMB 59051
350 Fifth Ave, 59th Floor
New York, NY 10118

Published by Crabtree Publishing Company in 2018

First Published by Book Life in 2017
Copyright © 2017 Book Life

Author: Steffi Cavell-Clarke

Editors: Charlie Ogden, Janine Deschenes

Design: Natalie Carr

Proofreader: Petrice Custance

Production coordinator and prepress technician (interior): Margaret Amy Salter

Prepress technician (covers): Ken Wright

Print coordinator: Margaret Amy Salter

Photographs

iStock: Wavebreakmedia p 6; asiseeit pp 7, 8, 21, 22 (top left) (bottom left); FatCamera p 13

All other images from Shutterstock

Printed in the USA/072017/CG20170524

Library and Archives Canada Cataloguing in Publication

Cavell-Clarke, Steffi, author
    Helping others / Steffi Cavell-Clarke.

(Our values)
Includes index.
Issued in print and electronic formats.
ISBN 978-0-7787-3703-2 (hardcover).--
ISBN 978-0-7787-3876-3 (softcover).--
ISBN 978-1-4271-1985-8 (HTML)

    1. Helping behavior--Juvenile literature. I. Title.

BF723.H45C38 2017   j158.3   C2017-902505-8
                                            C2017-902506-6

Library of Congress Cataloging-in-Publication Data

Names: Cavell-Clarke, Steffi, author.
Title: Helping others / Steffi Cavell-Clarke.
Description: New York : Crabtree Publishing Company, [2018] |
  Series: Our values | Audience: Age: 8-11. | Audience: K to Grade 3. |
  Includes index.
Identifiers: LCCN 2017016731 (print) | LCCN 2017020682 (ebook) |
  ISBN 9781427119858 (Electronic HTML) |
  ISBN 9780778737032 (reinforced library binding) |
  ISBN 9780778738763 (pbk.)
Subjects: LCSH: Helping behavior--Juvenile literature.
Classification: LCC BF637.H4 (ebook) | LCC BF637.H4 C388 2018 (print)
  | DDC 177/.7--dc23
LC record available at https://lccn.loc.gov/2017016731

CONTENTS

Words that look like **this** can be found in the glossary on page 24.

WHAT ARE VALUES?

Values are the things that you believe are important, such as being a good friend. The ways we think and behave depend on our values. Values teach us how we should **respect** each other and ourselves. Sharing the same values with others helps us work and live together in a **community**.

Working together with others

Respecting others

Understanding different faiths

Values make our communities better places to live. Think about the values in your community. What is important to you and the people around you?

Telling the truth

Respecting the law

Listening to others

5

HELPING OTHERS

To help someone means to offer them your time and assistance when they are in need. Helping someone often means that you have empathy for them, or put yourself in their shoes.

You can help others in a lot of different ways. Perhaps your teacher needs help putting away equipment after gym class. You can help your parents and **siblings** at home by doing your chores. A local **charity** may need your help with **donations,** such as winter clothing for those in need.

WHY IS HELPING IMPORTANT?

When you help people in your communities, such as at home, school, and in your neighborhood, you make them safer, cleaner, and better places to live, learn, and play.

Helping someone is a kind and friendly thing to do. It shows them that you respect and care about them.

Helping others can also make you feel good! When you help others, you are treating them the way you want to be treated. Everyone needs help sometimes. If you help others, they are likely to help you in return.

ASKING FOR HELP

It is very important that we ask others for help when we need it. You can ask your parents or **guardians**, teachers, close friends, and other trusted adults for help.

We ask for help for many reasons. You might have a problem that you can't solve by yourself. You might have hurt yourself, feel sick, or have lost your favorite toy. It is good to sometimes rely on others for help.

Damian feels frustrated because he is having trouble understanding a science question. He asks Andrew to help him.

Andrew sits with Damian and explains the question to him. Damian feels much more **confident** after asking for help.

11

PEOPLE WHO HELP US

There are people who live in our community whose job it is to help us. They make our communities safe places to live. Police officers, firefighters, doctors, and nurses are able to help us in an **emergency**.

Nurse

Firefighter

Police Officer

Doctor

You can ask any of these community helpers for help when you need it. You should also help these people by acting **responsibly** and staying safe, such as by following rules when you cross the road. It is very important that we help keep each other safe, too. You can help your friends by telling them if you think they are doing something unsafe.

LISTENING TO OTHERS

When people need help, they often talk to others about it. It is important to listen to other people. Listening to other people can help you to understand what they are thinking and feeling. Ask someone how they need your help and listen to their answer.

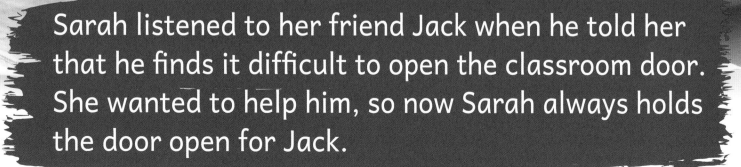

Sarah listened to her friend Jack when he told her that he finds it difficult to open the classroom door. She wanted to help him, so now Sarah always holds the door open for Jack.

15

HELPING OTHERS AT SCHOOL

It is important that we help others at school. We can help teachers by being quiet when they are talking, and by following the classroom rules. This also helps you and your classmates learn in a quiet, safe environment.

Teachers help us learn new things at school. They teach us about subjects such as math, science, and how to read and write. They can also teach us important lessons such as how to respect others and ourselves.

Helping teachers will make their day easier. By helping them, you help yourself learn!

HELPING OTHERS AT HOME

Family members, such as parents, guardians, and siblings, all have a role to play to care for and help their families. Parents and guardians often work very hard to care for their family. You can make their day easier by offering to help.

If you would like to help but don't know how to do something, just ask!

There are many ways you can help at home. Being kind to your family members or doing your chores helps make your home a good place to live. Matt tidies his bedroom to help his mom. He also sets the table for dinner while his dad is cooking.

19

HELPING OUR COMMUNITIES

We can help our community by helping the **environment**. We can do this by throwing our garbage in a garbage can, recycling, and **reusing** shopping bags. This helps keep Earth a safe place to live.

We all live on Earth, which makes us all part of a global community. Some charities help people in need around the world. You can help others in your global community by volunteering to help a charity.

Charities also help others in our local communities. Jamie helps others in her city by donating extra food to a charity that gives meals to those who need it.

MAKING A DIFFERENCE

Helping others makes your communities better places to live, work, and play. Try out some of these today!

Help carry shopping bags.

Hold the door open.

Help keep your neighborhood clean.

Volunteer with a charity.

Help others be safe.

Even though it is nice to help others, you still need to keep yourself safe. Remember to always tell a parent or guardian before speaking to or helping a stranger.

GLOSSARY

charity [CHAR-i-tee] A fund or institution that helps people in need
community [kuh-MYOO-ni-tee] A group of people who live, work, and play in a place
confident [KON-fi-duh nt] A feeling that you can do something well
donation [doh-NEY-shuh n] A gift of money or goods
emergency [ih-MUR-juh n-see] A dangerous problem that happens suddenly
environment [en-VAHY-ruh n-muh nt] Nature or the natural world
guardian [GAHR-dee-uh n] A person who looks after something or someone
law [law] Rules made by government that a community has to follow
respect [ri-SPEKT] The act of giving something or someone the attention it deserves; believing something or someone is important
responsible [ri-spon-suh-buhl] Reliable or dependable
reusing [re yooz ing] Using something more than once
siblings [SIB-lings] Brothers and sisters

INDEX